# 2019
# Instrumental Practice
# Journal

Name _____

If Found, Please Call:_____

E-mail: _____

# Goals

My 5-year goals with my instrument are: (be as specific as possible):

1._____
2._____
3._____
4._____
5._____

## My 3-year goals with my instrument are:

1._____
2._____
3._____
4._____
5._____

## My goals with my instrument for this year are:

1._____
2._____
3._____
4._____
5._____

My goals for January-March are (complete before 1/1/19):

1._____
2._____
3._____
4._____
5._____

My goals for April-June are (complete before 4/1/19):

1._____
2._____
3._____
4._____
5._____

My goals for June-August are (complete before 6/1/19):

1._____
2._____
3._____
4._____
5._____

My goals for September-December are (complete before 9/1/19):

1._____
2._____
3._____
4._____
5._____

# Repertoire

## Repertoire Studied

1._____
2._____
3._____
4._____
5._____
6._____

## Technical Studies

1._____
2._____
3._____
4._____
5._____
6._____

## Repertoire I'd like to learn:

1._____
2._____
3._____
4._____
5._____
6._____

# Public Performances:

| Date | Performance Name | Location |
|------|------------------|----------|
| 1. | | |
| 2. | | |
| 3. | | |
| 4. | | |
| 5. | | |
| 6. | | |
| 7. | | |
| 8. | | |
| 9. | | |
| 10. | | |

# Notes, questions, telephone numbers

| Sample | Assignments for this week | Monday | Tuesday | Wednesday | Thursday |
|---|---|---|---|---|---|
| **Long Tones/ Scale Studies** | 1.*Long Tones w/tuner*<br>2.*Klose Scales*<br>3.*Baerman Studies*<br>4. | 1. 7:30-8:00<br>2. 8:00-8:15<br>3. 8:15-8:45 | 1. 7:00-7:30<br>2. 7:30-7:45<br>3. 7:45-8:15 | 1. 7:30-8:00<br>2. 8:00-8:15<br>3. 8:15-8:45 | 1. 7:30-8:00<br>2. 8:00-8:15<br>3. 8:15-8:45 |
| **Technical Studies** | 1.*Opperman Studies*<br>2.<br>3.<br>4. | 1. 10:00-10:15 | 1. 10:00-10:15 | | 1. 10:00-10:15 |
| **Etudes** | 1.*Rose No. 34*<br>2.*Jeanjean No. 2*<br>3.<br>4. | 1. 10:15-10:30<br>2. 10:30-11:00 | | 1. 10:15-10:30<br>2. 10:30-11:00 | 1. 10:15-10:30<br>2. 10:30-11:00 |
| **Repertoire** | 1.*Poulenc Sonata*<br>2.*Nielsen Concerto*<br>3.*Brahms Sonata*<br>4. | 1. 11:00-11:30<br>2. 11:30-12:00 | 2. 11:00-12:00 | 3. 11:15-12:00 | 1. 11:00-11:15<br>2. 11:15-12:00 |
| **Excerpts** | 1.*Stravinsky Rite of Spr.*<br>2.*Mahler Symphony No. 1*<br>3.*Tchaikowsky Symph. 5*<br>4. | | 1. 12:00-12:15<br>2. 12:15-12:30<br>3. 12:30-1:00 | 1. 12:00-12:15<br>2. 12:15-12:30<br>3. 12:30-1:00 | 1. 12:00-12:15<br>2. 12:15-12:30<br>3. 12:30-1:00 |
| **Totals** | | *3:45* | *4:00* | *3:45* | *4:45* |

| Sample | Friday | Saturday | Sunday | Totals | Questions |
|---|---|---|---|---|---|
| Long Tones/ Scale Studies | 1. 7:00-7:30<br>2. 7:30-7:45<br>3. 7:45-8:15 | 1. 8:00-8:30<br>2. 8:30-8:45<br>3. 8:45-9:15 | 1. 8:00-8:30<br>2. 8:30-8:45<br>3. 8:45-9:15 | 1. 3:30<br>2. 1:45<br>3. 3:30 | |
| Technical Studies | 1. 10:00-10:15 | | | 1. 1:00 | |
| Etudes | | 1. 10:15-10:30<br>2. 10:30-11:00 | | 1. 1:00<br>2. 2:00 | |
| Repertoire | 3. 10:15-10:45 | 2: 11:00-12:00 | 3:10:00-11:00 | 1. 0:45<br>2. 3:15<br>3. 2:15 | |
| Excerpts | | 1. 12:00-12:15<br>2. 12:15-12:30<br>3. 12:30-1:00 | | 1. 1:00<br>2. 1:00<br>3. 2:00 | |
| | 2:45 | 4:00 | 2:15 | 25:15 | |

| December 31, 2018 | Assignments for this week | Monday | Tuesday | Wednesday | Thursday |
|---|---|---|---|---|---|
| Long Tones/ Scale Studies | 1.<br>2.<br>3.<br>4. | | | | |
| Technical Studies | 1.<br>2.<br>3.<br>4. | | | | |
| Etudes | 1.<br>2.<br>3.<br>4. | | | | |
| Repertoire | 1.<br>2.<br>3.<br>4. | | | | |
| Excerpts | 1.<br>2.<br>3.<br>4. | | | | |
| Totals | | | | | |

| January 4, 2019 | Friday | Saturday | Sunday | Totals | Questions |
|---|---|---|---|---|---|
| Long Tones/ Scale Studies | | | | | |
| Technical Studies | | | | | |
| Etudes | | | | | |
| Repertoire | | | | | |
| Excerpts | | | | | |
| | | | | | |

| January 7, 2019 | Assignments for this week | Monday | Tuesday | Wednesday | Thursday |
|---|---|---|---|---|---|
| Long Tones/ Scale Studies | 1.<br>2.<br>3.<br>4. | | | | |
| Technical Studies | 1.<br>2.<br>3.<br>4. | | | | |
| Etudes | 1.<br>2.<br>3.<br>4. | | | | |
| Repertoire | 1.<br>2.<br>3.<br>4. | | | | |
| Excerpts | 1.<br>2.<br>3.<br>4. | | | | |
| Totals | | | | | |

| January 11, 2019 | Friday | Saturday | Sunday | Totals | Questions |
|---|---|---|---|---|---|
| Long Tones/ Scale Studies | | | | | |
| Technical Studies | | | | | |
| Etudes | | | | | |
| Repertoire | | | | | |
| Excerpts | | | | | |
| | | | | | |

| January 14, 2019 | Assignments for this week | Monday | Tuesday | Wednesday | Thursday |
|---|---|---|---|---|---|
| Long Tones/ Scale Studies | 1.<br>2.<br>3.<br>4. | | | | |
| Technical Studies | 1.<br>2.<br>3.<br>4. | | | | |
| Etudes | 1.<br>2.<br>3.<br>4. | | | | |
| Repertoire | 1.<br>2.<br>3.<br>4. | | | | |
| Excerpts | 1.<br>2.<br>3.<br>4. | | | | |
| Totals | | | | | |

| January 18, 2019 | Friday | Saturday | Sunday | Totals | Questions |
|---|---|---|---|---|---|
| Long Tones/ Scale Studies | | | | | |
| Technical Studies | | | | | |
| Etudes | | | | | |
| Repertoire | | | | | |
| Excerpts | | | | | |
| | | | | | |

| January 21, 2019 | Assignments for this week | Monday | Tuesday | Wednesday | Thursday |
|---|---|---|---|---|---|
| Long Tones/ Scale Studies | 1.<br>2.<br>3.<br>4. | | | | |
| Technical Studies | 1.<br>2.<br>3.<br>4. | | | | |
| Etudes | 1.<br>2.<br>3.<br>4. | | | | |
| Repertoire | 1.<br>2.<br>3.<br>4. | | | | |
| Excerpts | 1.<br>2.<br>3.<br>4. | | | | |
| Totals | | | | | |

| January 25, 2019 | Friday | Saturday | Sunday | Totals | Questions |
|---|---|---|---|---|---|
| Long Tones/ Scale Studies | | | | | |
| Technical Studies | | | | | |
| Etudes | | | | | |
| Repertoire | | | | | |
| Excerpts | | | | | |
| | | | | | |

| January 28, 2019 | Assignments for this week | Monday | Tuesday | Wednesday | Thursday |
|---|---|---|---|---|---|
| Long Tones/ Scale Studies | 1.<br>2.<br>3.<br>4. | | | | |
| Technical Studies | 1.<br>2.<br>3.<br>4. | | | | |
| Etudes | 1.<br>2.<br>3.<br>4. | | | | |
| Repertoire | 1.<br>2.<br>3.<br>4. | | | | |
| Excerpts | 1.<br>2.<br>3.<br>4. | | | | |
| Totals | | | | | |

| February 1, 2019 | Friday | Saturday | Sunday | Totals | Questions |
|---|---|---|---|---|---|
| Long Tones/<br>Scale Studies | | | | | |
| Technical Studies | | | | | |
| Etudes | | | | | |
| Repertoire | | | | | |
| Excerpts | | | | | |
| | | | | | |

| February 4, 2019 | Assignments for this week | Monday | Tuesday | Wednesday | Thursday |
|---|---|---|---|---|---|
| Long Tones/ Scale Studies | 1.<br>2.<br>3.<br>4. | | | | |
| Technical Studies | 1.<br>2.<br>3.<br>4. | | | | |
| Etudes | 1.<br>2.<br>3.<br>4. | | | | |
| Repertoire | 1.<br>2.<br>3.<br>4. | | | | |
| Excerpts | 1.<br>2.<br>3.<br>4. | | | | |
| Totals | | | | | |

| February 8, 2019 | Friday | Saturday | Sunday | Totals | Questions |
|---|---|---|---|---|---|
| Long Tones/ Scale Studies | | | | | |
| Technical Studies | | | | | |
| Etudes | | | | | |
| Repertoire | | | | | |
| Excerpts | | | | | |
| | | | | | |

| February 11, 2019 | Assignments for this week | Monday | Tuesday | Wednesday | Thursday |
|---|---|---|---|---|---|
| Long Tones/ Scale Studies | 1.<br>2.<br>3.<br>4. | | | | |
| Technical Studies | 1.<br>2.<br>3.<br>4. | | | | |
| Etudes | 1.<br>2.<br>3.<br>4. | | | | |
| Repertoire | 1.<br>2.<br>3.<br>4. | | | | |
| Excerpts | 1.<br>2.<br>3.<br>4. | | | | |
| Totals | | | | | |

| February 15, 2019 | Friday | Saturday | Sunday | Totals | Questions |
|---|---|---|---|---|---|
| Long Tones/ Scale Studies | | | | | |
| Technical Studies | | | | | |
| Etudes | | | | | |
| Repertoire | | | | | |
| Excerpts | | | | | |
| | | | | | |

| February 18, 2019 | Assignments for this week | Monday | Tuesday | Wednesday | Thursday |
|---|---|---|---|---|---|
| Long Tones/ Scale Studies | 1.<br>2.<br>3.<br>4. | | | | |
| Technical Studies | 1.<br>2.<br>3.<br>4. | | | | |
| Etudes | 1.<br>2.<br>3.<br>4. | | | | |
| Repertoire | 1.<br>2.<br>3.<br>4. | | | | |
| Excerpts | 1.<br>2.<br>3.<br>4. | | | | |
| Totals | | | | | |

| February 22, 2019 | Friday | Saturday | Sunday | Totals | Questions |
|---|---|---|---|---|---|
| Long Tones/ Scale Studies | | | | | |
| Technical Studies | | | | | |
| Etudes | | | | | |
| Repertoire | | | | | |
| Excerpts | | | | | |
| | | | | | |

| February 25, 2019 | Assignments for this week | Monday | Tuesday | Wednesday | Thursday |
|---|---|---|---|---|---|
| Long Tones/ Scale Studies | 1.<br>2.<br>3.<br>4. | | | | |
| Technical Studies | 1.<br>2.<br>3.<br>4. | | | | |
| Etudes | 1.<br>2.<br>3.<br>4. | | | | |
| Repertoire | 1.<br>2.<br>3.<br>4. | | | | |
| Excerpts | 1.<br>2.<br>3.<br>4. | | | | |
| Totals | | | | | |

| March 1, 2019 | Friday | Saturday | Sunday | Totals | Questions |
|---|---|---|---|---|---|
| Long Tones/ Scale Studies | | | | | |
| Technical Studies | | | | | |
| Etudes | | | | | |
| Repertoire | | | | | |
| Excerpts | | | | | |
| | | | | | |

| March 4, 2019 | Assignments for this week | Monday | Tuesday | Wednesday | Thursday |
|---|---|---|---|---|---|
| Long Tones/ Scale Studies | 1.<br>2.<br>3.<br>4. | | | | |
| Technical Studies | 1.<br>2.<br>3.<br>4. | | | | |
| Etudes | 1.<br>2.<br>3.<br>4. | | | | |
| Repertoire | 1.<br>2.<br>3.<br>4. | | | | |
| Excerpts | 1.<br>2.<br>3.<br>4. | | | | |
| Totals | | | | | |

Month to date total:_____

Year to date total_____

| March 8, 2019 | Friday | Saturday | Sunday | Totals | Questions |
|---|---|---|---|---|---|
| Long Tones/ Scale Studies | | | | | |
| Technical Studies | | | | | |
| Etudes | | | | | |
| Repertoire | | | | | |
| Excerpts | | | | | |
| | | | | | |

| March 11, 2019 | Assignments for this week | Monday | Tuesday | Wednesday | Thursday |
|---|---|---|---|---|---|
| Long Tones/ Scale Studies | 1.<br>2.<br>3.<br>4. | | | | |
| Technical Studies | 1.<br>2.<br>3.<br>4. | | | | |
| Etudes | 1.<br>2.<br>3.<br>4. | | | | |
| Repertoire | 1.<br>2.<br>3.<br>4. | | | | |
| Excerpts | 1.<br>2.<br>3.<br>4. | | | | |
| Totals | | | | | |

| March 15, 2019 | Friday | Saturday | Sunday | Totals | Questions |
|---|---|---|---|---|---|
| Long Tones/<br>Scale Studies | | | | | |
| Technical Studies | | | | | |
| Etudes | | | | | |
| Repertoire | | | | | |
| Excerpts | | | | | |
| | | | | | |

| March 18, 2019 | Assignments for this week | Monday | Tuesday | Wednesday | Thursday |
|---|---|---|---|---|---|
| Long Tones/ Scale Studies | 1.<br>2.<br>3.<br>4. | | | | |
| Technical Studies | 1.<br>2.<br>3.<br>4. | | | | |
| Etudes | 1.<br>2.<br>3.<br>4. | | | | |
| Repertoire | 1.<br>2.<br>3.<br>4. | | | | |
| Excerpts | 1.<br>2.<br>3.<br>4. | | | | |
| Totals | | | | | |

| March 22, 2019 | Friday | Saturday | Sunday | Totals | Questions |
|---|---|---|---|---|---|
| Long Tones/<br>Scale Studies | | | | | |
| Technical Studies | | | | | |
| Etudes | | | | | |
| Repertoire | | | | | |
| Excerpts | | | | | |
| | | | | | |

| March 25, 2019 | Assignments for this week | Monday | Tuesday | Wednesday | Thursday |
|---|---|---|---|---|---|
| Long Tones/ Scale Studies | 1.<br>2.<br>3.<br>4. | | | | |
| Technical Studies | 1.<br>2.<br>3.<br>4. | | | | |
| Etudes | 1.<br>2.<br>3.<br>4. | | | | |
| Repertoire | 1.<br>2.<br>3.<br>4. | | | | |
| Excerpts | 1.<br>2.<br>3.<br>4. | | | | |
| Totals | | | | | |

| March 29, 2019 | Friday | Saturday | Sunday | Totals | Questions |
|---|---|---|---|---|---|
| Long Tones/<br>Scale Studies | | | | | |
| Technical Studies | | | | | |
| Etudes | | | | | |
| Repertoire | | | | | |
| Excerpts | | | | | |
| | | | | | |

| April 1, 2019 | Assignments for this week | Monday | Tuesday | Wednesday | Thursday |
|---|---|---|---|---|---|
| **Long Tones/ Scale Studies** | 1.<br>2.<br>3.<br>4. | | | | |
| **Technical Studies** | 1.<br>2.<br>3.<br>4. | | | | |
| **Etudes** | 1.<br>2.<br>3.<br>4. | | | | |
| **Repertoire** | 1.<br>2.<br>3.<br>4. | | | | |
| **Excerpts** | 1.<br>2.<br>3.<br>4. | | | | |
| **Totals** | | | | | |

| April 5, 2019 | Friday | Saturday | Sunday | Totals | Questions |
|---|---|---|---|---|---|
| Long Tones/ Scale Studies | | | | | |
| Technical Studies | | | | | |
| Etudes | | | | | |
| Repertoire | | | | | |
| Excerpts | | | | | |
| | | | | | |

| April 8, 2019 | Assignments for this week | Monday | Tuesday | Wednesday | Thursday |
|---|---|---|---|---|---|
| Long Tones/ Scale Studies | 1.<br>2.<br>3.<br>4. | | | | |
| Technical Studies | 1.<br>2.<br>3.<br>4. | | | | |
| Etudes | 1.<br>2.<br>3.<br>4. | | | | |
| Repertoire | 1.<br>2.<br>3.<br>4. | | | | |
| Excerpts | 1.<br>2.<br>3.<br>4. | | | | |
| Totals | | | | | |

| April 12, 2019 | Friday | Saturday | Sunday | Totals | Questions |
|---|---|---|---|---|---|
| Long Tones/ Scale Studies | | | | | |
| Technical Studies | | | | | |
| Etudes | | | | | |
| Repertoire | | | | | |
| Excerpts | | | | | |
| | | | | | |

| April 15, 2019 | Assignments for this week | Monday | Tuesday | Wednesday | Thursday |
|---|---|---|---|---|---|
| Long Tones/ Scale Studies | 1.<br>2.<br>3.<br>4. | | | | |
| Technical Studies | 1.<br>2.<br>3.<br>4. | | | | |
| Etudes | 1.<br>2.<br>3.<br>4. | | | | |
| Repertoire | 1.<br>2.<br>3.<br>4. | | | | |
| Excerpts | 1.<br>2.<br>3.<br>4. | | | | |
| Totals | | | | | |

| April 19, 2019 | Friday | Saturday | Sunday | Totals | Questions |
|---|---|---|---|---|---|
| Long Tones/ Scale Studies | | | | | |
| Technical Studies | | | | | |
| Etudes | | | | | |
| Repertoire | | | | | |
| Excerpts | | | | | |
| | | | | | |

| April 22, 2019 | Assignments for this week | Monday | Tuesday | Wednesday | Thursday |
|---|---|---|---|---|---|
| Long Tones/ Scale Studies | 1.<br>2.<br>3.<br>4. | | | | |
| Technical Studies | 1.<br>2.<br>3.<br>4. | | | | |
| Etudes | 1.<br>2.<br>3.<br>4. | | | | |
| Repertoire | 1.<br>2.<br>3.<br>4. | | | | |
| Excerpts | 1.<br>2.<br>3.<br>4. | | | | |
| Totals | | | | | |

| April 26, 2019 | Friday | Saturday | Sunday | Totals | Questions |
|---|---|---|---|---|---|
| Long Tones/ Scale Studies | | | | | |
| Technical Studies | | | | | |
| Etudes | | | | | |
| Repertoire | | | | | |
| Excerpts | | | | | |
| | | | | | |

| April 29, 2019 | Assignments for this week | Monday | Tuesday | Wednesday | Thursday |
|---|---|---|---|---|---|
| Long Tones/ Scale Studies | 1.<br>2.<br>3.<br>4. | | | | |
| Technical Studies | 1.<br>2.<br>3.<br>4. | | | | |
| Etudes | 1.<br>2.<br>3.<br>4. | | | | |
| Repertoire | 1.<br>2.<br>3.<br>4. | | | | |
| Excerpts | 1.<br>2.<br>3.<br>4. | | | | |
| Totals | | | | | |

| May 3, 2019 | Friday | Saturday | Sunday | Totals | Questions |
|---|---|---|---|---|---|
| Long Tones/ Scale Studies | | | | | |
| Technical Studies | | | | | |
| Etudes | | | | | |
| Repertoire | | | | | |
| Excerpts | | | | | |
| | | | | | |

| May 6, 2019 | Assignments for this week | Monday | Tuesday | Wednesday | Thursday |
|---|---|---|---|---|---|
| Long Tones/ Scale Studies | 1.<br>2.<br>3.<br>4. | | | | |
| Technical Studies | 1.<br>2.<br>3.<br>4. | | | | |
| Etudes | 1.<br>2.<br>3.<br>4. | | | | |
| Repertoire | 1.<br>2.<br>3.<br>4. | | | | |
| Excerpts | 1.<br>2.<br>3.<br>4. | | | | |
| Totals | | | | | |

| May 10, 2019 | Friday | Saturday | Sunday | Totals | Questions |
|---|---|---|---|---|---|
| Long Tones/ Scale Studies | | | | | |
| Technical Studies | | | | | |
| Etudes | | | | | |
| Repertoire | | | | | |
| Excerpts | | | | | |
| | | | | | |

| May 13, 2019 | Assignments for this week | Monday | Tuesday | Wednesday | Thursday |
|---|---|---|---|---|---|
| Long Tones/ Scale Studies | 1.<br>2.<br>3.<br>4. | | | | |
| Technical Studies | 1.<br>2.<br>3.<br>4. | | | | |
| Etudes | 1.<br>2.<br>3.<br>4. | | | | |
| Repertoire | 1.<br>2.<br>3.<br>4. | | | | |
| Excerpts | 1.<br>2.<br>3.<br>4. | | | | |
| Totals | | | | | |

| May 17, 2019 | Friday | Saturday | Sunday | Totals | Questions |
|---|---|---|---|---|---|
| Long Tones/ Scale Studies | | | | | |
| Technical Studies | | | | | |
| Etudes | | | | | |
| Repertoire | | | | | |
| Excerpts | | | | | |
| | | | | | |

| May 20, 2019 | Assignments for this week | Monday | Tuesday | Wednesday | Thursday |
|---|---|---|---|---|---|
| Long Tones/ Scale Studies | 1.<br>2.<br>3.<br>4. | | | | |
| Technical Studies | 1.<br>2.<br>3.<br>4. | | | | |
| Etudes | 1.<br>2.<br>3.<br>4. | | | | |
| Repertoire | 1.<br>2.<br>3.<br>4. | | | | |
| Excerpts | 1.<br>2.<br>3.<br>4. | | | | |
| Totals | | | | | |

| May 24, 2019 | Friday | Saturday | Sunday | Totals | Questions |
|---|---|---|---|---|---|
| Long Tones/ Scale Studies | | | | | |
| Technical Studies | | | | | |
| Etudes | | | | | |
| Repertoire | | | | | |
| Excerpts | | | | | |
| | | | | | |

| May 27, 2019 | Assignments for this week | Monday | Tuesday | Wednesday | Thursday |
|---|---|---|---|---|---|
| Long Tones/ Scale Studies | 1.<br>2.<br>3.<br>4. | | | | |
| Technical Studies | 1.<br>2.<br>3.<br>4. | | | | |
| Etudes | 1.<br>2.<br>3.<br>4. | | | | |
| Repertoire | 1.<br>2.<br>3.<br>4. | | | | |
| Excerpts | 1.<br>2.<br>3.<br>4. | | | | |
| Totals | | | | | |

| May 31, 2019 | Friday | Saturday | Sunday | Totals | Questions |
|---|---|---|---|---|---|
| Long Tones/ Scale Studies | | | | | |
| Technical Studies | | | | | |
| Etudes | | | | | |
| Repertoire | | | | | |
| Excerpts | | | | | |
| | | | | | |

| June 3, 2019 | Assignments for this week | Monday | Tuesday | Wednesday | Thursday |
|---|---|---|---|---|---|
| Long Tones/ Scale Studies | 1.<br>2.<br>3.<br>4. | | | | |
| Technical Studies | 1.<br>2.<br>3.<br>4. | | | | |
| Etudes | 1.<br>2.<br>3.<br>4. | | | | |
| Repertoire | 1.<br>2.<br>3.<br>4. | | | | |
| Excerpts | 1.<br>2.<br>3.<br>4. | | | | |
| Totals | | | | | |

| June 7, 2019 | Friday | Saturday | Sunday | Totals | Questions |
|---|---|---|---|---|---|
| Long Tones/ Scale Studies | | | | | |
| Technical Studies | | | | | |
| Etudes | | | | | |
| Repertoire | | | | | |
| Excerpts | | | | | |
| | | | | | |

| June 10, 2019 | Assignments for this week | Monday | Tuesday | Wednesday | Thursday |
|---|---|---|---|---|---|
| **Long Tones/ Scale Studies** | 1.<br>2.<br>3.<br>4. | | | | |
| Technical Studies | 1.<br>2.<br>3.<br>4. | | | | |
| **Etudes** | 1.<br>2.<br>3.<br>4. | | | | |
| **Repertoire** | 1.<br>2.<br>3.<br>4. | | | | |
| **Excerpts** | 1.<br>2.<br>3.<br>4. | | | | |
| **Totals** | | | | | |

| June 14, 2019 | Friday | Saturday | Sunday | Totals | Questions |
|---|---|---|---|---|---|
| Long Tones/ Scale Studies | | | | | |
| Technical Studies | | | | | |
| Etudes | | | | | |
| Repertoire | | | | | |
| Excerpts | | | | | |
| | | | | | |

| June 17, 2019 | Assignments for this week | Monday | Tuesday | Wednesday | Thursday |
|---|---|---|---|---|---|
| Long Tones/ Scale Studies | 1.<br>2.<br>3.<br>4. | | | | |
| Technical Studies | 1.<br>2.<br>3.<br>4. | | | | |
| Etudes | 1.<br>2.<br>3.<br>4. | | | | |
| Repertoire | 1.<br>2.<br>3.<br>4. | | | | |
| Excerpts | 1.<br>2.<br>3.<br>4. | | | | |
| Totals | | | | | |

| June 21, 2019 | Friday | Saturday | Sunday | Totals | Questions |
|---|---|---|---|---|---|
| Long Tones/ Scale Studies | | | | | |
| Technical Studies | | | | | |
| Etudes | | | | | |
| Repertoire | | | | | |
| Excerpts | | | | | |
| | | | | | |

| June 24, 2019 | Assignments for this week | Monday | Tuesday | Wednesday | Thursday |
|---|---|---|---|---|---|
| Long Tones/ Scale Studies | 1.<br>2.<br>3.<br>4. | | | | |
| Technical Studies | 1.<br>2.<br>3.<br>4. | | | | |
| Etudes | 1.<br>2.<br>3.<br>4. | | | | |
| Repertoire | 1.<br>2.<br>3.<br>4. | | | | |
| Excerpts | 1.<br>2.<br>3.<br>4. | | | | |
| Totals | | | | | |

| June 28, 2019 | Friday | Saturday | Sunday | Totals | Questions |
|---|---|---|---|---|---|
| Long Tones/ Scale Studies | | | | | |
| Technical Studies | | | | | |
| Etudes | | | | | |
| Repertoire | | | | | |
| Excerpts | | | | | |
| | | | | | |

| July 1, 2019 | Assignments for this week | Monday | Tuesday | Wednesday | Thursday |
|---|---|---|---|---|---|
| Long Tones/ Scale Studies | 1.<br>2.<br>3.<br>4. | | | | |
| Technical Studies | 1.<br>2.<br>3.<br>4. | | | | |
| Etudes | 1.<br>2.<br>3.<br>4. | | | | |
| Repertoire | 1.<br>2.<br>3.<br>4. | | | | |
| Excerpts | 1.<br>2.<br>3.<br>4. | | | | |
| Totals | | | | | |

| July 5, 2019 | Friday | Saturday | Sunday | Totals | Questions |
|---|---|---|---|---|---|
| Long Tones/ Scale Studies | | | | | |
| Technical Studies | | | | | |
| Etudes | | | | | |
| Repertoire | | | | | |
| Excerpts | | | | | |
| | | | | | |

| July 8, 2019 | Assignments for this week | Monday | Tuesday | Wednesday | Thursday |
|---|---|---|---|---|---|
| Long Tones/ Scale Studies | 1.<br>2.<br>3.<br>4. | | | | |
| Technical Studies | 1.<br>2.<br>3.<br>4. | | | | |
| Etudes | 1.<br>2.<br>3.<br>4. | | | | |
| Repertoire | 1.<br>2.<br>3.<br>4. | | | | |
| Excerpts | 1.<br>2.<br>3.<br>4. | | | | |
| Totals | | | | | |

| July 12, 2019 | Friday | Saturday | Sunday | Totals | Questions |
|---|---|---|---|---|---|
| Long Tones/ Scale Studies | | | | | |
| Technical Studies | | | | | |
| Etudes | | | | | |
| Repertoire | | | | | |
| Excerpts | | | | | |
| | | | | | |

| July 15, 2019 | Assignments for this week | Monday | Tuesday | Wednesday | Thursday |
|---|---|---|---|---|---|
| Long Tones/ Scale Studies | 1.<br>2.<br>3.<br>4. | | | | |
| Technical Studies | 1.<br>2.<br>3.<br>4. | | | | |
| Etudes | 1.<br>2.<br>3.<br>4. | | | | |
| Repertoire | 1.<br>2.<br>3.<br>4. | | | | |
| Excerpts | 1.<br>2.<br>3.<br>4. | | | | |
| Totals | | | | | |

| July 19, 2019 | Friday | Saturday | Sunday | Totals | Questions |
|---|---|---|---|---|---|
| Long Tones/ Scale Studies | | | | | |
| Technical Studies | | | | | |
| Etudes | | | | | |
| Repertoire | | | | | |
| Excerpts | | | | | |
| | | | | | |

| July 22, 2019 | Assignments for this week | Monday | Tuesday | Wednesday | Thursday |
|---|---|---|---|---|---|
| Long Tones/ Scale Studies | 1.<br>2.<br>3.<br>4. | | | | |
| Technical Studies | 1.<br>2.<br>3.<br>4. | | | | |
| Etudes | 1.<br>2.<br>3.<br>4. | | | | |
| Repertoire | 1.<br>2.<br>3.<br>4. | | | | |
| Excerpts | 1.<br>2.<br>3.<br>4. | | | | |
| Totals | | | | | |

| July 26, 2019 | Friday | Saturday | Sunday | Totals | Questions |
|---|---|---|---|---|---|
| Long Tones/ Scale Studies | | | | | |
| Technical Studies | | | | | |
| Etudes | | | | | |
| Repertoire | | | | | |
| Excerpts | | | | | |
| | | | | | |

| July 29, 2019 | Assignments for this week | Monday | Tuesday | Wednesday | Thursday |
|---|---|---|---|---|---|
| Long Tones/ Scale Studies | 1.<br>2.<br>3.<br>4. | | | | |
| Technical Studies | 1.<br>2.<br>3.<br>4. | | | | |
| Etudes | 1.<br>2.<br>3.<br>4. | | | | |
| Repertoire | 1.<br>2.<br>3.<br>4. | | | | |
| Excerpts | 1.<br>2.<br>3.<br>4. | | | | |
| Totals | | | | | |

| August 2, 2019 | Friday | Saturday | Sunday | Totals | Questions |
|---|---|---|---|---|---|
| Long Tones/ Scale Studies | | | | | |
| Technical Studies | | | | | |
| Etudes | | | | | |
| Repertoire | | | | | |
| Excerpts | | | | | |
| | | | | | |

| August 5, 2019 | Assignments for this week | Monday | Tuesday | Wednesday | Thursday |
|---|---|---|---|---|---|
| Long Tones/ Scale Studies | 1.<br>2.<br>3.<br>4. | | | | |
| Technical Studies | 1.<br>2.<br>3.<br>4. | | | | |
| Etudes | 1.<br>2.<br>3.<br>4. | | | | |
| Repertoire | 1.<br>2.<br>3.<br>4. | | | | |
| Excerpts | 1.<br>2.<br>3.<br>4. | | | | |
| Totals | | | | | |

| August 9, 2019 | Friday | Saturday | Sunday | Totals | Questions |
|---|---|---|---|---|---|
| Long Tones/ Scale Studies | | | | | |
| Technical Studies | | | | | |
| Etudes | | | | | |
| Repertoire | | | | | |
| Excerpts | | | | | |
| | | | | | |

| August 12, 2019 | Assignments for this week | Monday | Tuesday | Wednesday | Thursday |
|---|---|---|---|---|---|
| Long Tones/ Scale Studies | 1.<br>2.<br>3.<br>4. | | | | |
| Technical Studies | 1.<br>2.<br>3.<br>4. | | | | |
| Etudes | 1.<br>2.<br>3.<br>4. | | | | |
| Repertoire | 1.<br>2.<br>3.<br>4. | | | | |
| Excerpts | 1.<br>2.<br>3.<br>4. | | | | |
| Totals | | | | | |

| August 16, 2019 | Friday | Saturday | Sunday | Totals | Questions |
|---|---|---|---|---|---|
| Long Tones/ Scale Studies | | | | | |
| Technical Studies | | | | | |
| Etudes | | | | | |
| Repertoire | | | | | |
| Excerpts | | | | | |
| | | | | | |

| August 19, 2019 | Assignments for this week | Monday | Tuesday | Wednesday | Thursday |
|---|---|---|---|---|---|
| Long Tones/ Scale Studies | 1.<br>2.<br>3.<br>4. | | | | |
| Technical Studies | 1.<br>2.<br>3.<br>4. | | | | |
| Etudes | 1.<br>2.<br>3.<br>4. | | | | |
| Repertoire | 1.<br>2.<br>3.<br>4. | | | | |
| Excerpts | 1.<br>2.<br>3.<br>4. | | | | |
| Totals | | | | | |

| August 23, 2019 | Friday | Saturday | Sunday | Totals | Questions |
|---|---|---|---|---|---|
| Long Tones/ Scale Studies | | | | | |
| Technical Studies | | | | | |
| Etudes | | | | | |
| Repertoire | | | | | |
| Excerpts | | | | | |
| | | | | | |

| August 26, 2019 | Assignments for this week | Monday | Tuesday | Wednesday | Thursday |
|---|---|---|---|---|---|
| Long Tones/ Scale Studies | 1.<br>2.<br>3.<br>4. | | | | |
| Technical Studies | 1.<br>2.<br>3.<br>4. | | | | |
| Etudes | 1.<br>2.<br>3.<br>4. | | | | |
| Repertoire | 1.<br>2.<br>3.<br>4. | | | | |
| Excerpts | 1.<br>2.<br>3.<br>4. | | | | |
| Totals | | | | | |

| August 30, 2019 | Friday | Saturday | Sunday | Totals | Questions |
|---|---|---|---|---|---|
| Long Tones/ Scale Studies | | | | | |
| Technical Studies | | | | | |
| Etudes | | | | | |
| Repertoire | | | | | |
| Excerpts | | | | | |
| | | | | | |

Month to date total:_____

Year to date total_____

| September 2, 2019 | Assignments for this week | Monday | Tuesday | Wednesday | Thursday |
|---|---|---|---|---|---|
| Long Tones/ Scale Studies | 1.<br>2.<br>3.<br>4. | | | | |
| Technical Studies | 1.<br>2.<br>3.<br>4. | | | | |
| Etudes | 1.<br>2.<br>3.<br>4. | | | | |
| Repertoire | 1.<br>2.<br>3.<br>4. | | | | |
| Excerpts | 1.<br>2.<br>3.<br>4. | | | | |
| Totals | | | | | |

| September 6, 2019 | Friday | Saturday | Sunday | Totals | Questions |
|---|---|---|---|---|---|
| Long Tones/ Scale Studies | | | | | |
| Technical Studies | | | | | |
| Etudes | | | | | |
| Repertoire | | | | | |
| Excerpts | | | | | |
| | | | | | |

| September 9, 2019 | Assignments for this week | Monday | Tuesday | Wednesday | Thursday |
|---|---|---|---|---|---|
| Long Tones/ Scale Studies | 1.<br>2.<br>3.<br>4. | | | | |
| Technical Studies | 1.<br>2.<br>3.<br>4. | | | | |
| Etudes | 1.<br>2.<br>3.<br>4. | | | | |
| Repertoire | 1.<br>2.<br>3.<br>4. | | | | |
| Excerpts | 1.<br>2.<br>3.<br>4. | | | | |
| Totals | | | | | |

| September 13, 2019 | Friday | Saturday | Sunday | Totals | Questions |
|---|---|---|---|---|---|
| Long Tones/ Scale Studies | | | | | |
| Technical Studies | | | | | |
| Etudes | | | | | |
| Repertoire | | | | | |
| Excerpts | | | | | |
| | | | | | |

| September 16, 2019 | Assignments for this week | Monday | Tuesday | Wednesday | Thursday |
|---|---|---|---|---|---|
| Long Tones/ Scale Studies | 1.<br>2.<br>3.<br>4. | | | | |
| Technical Studies | 1.<br>2.<br>3.<br>4. | | | | |
| Etudes | 1.<br>2.<br>3.<br>4. | | | | |
| Repertoire | 1.<br>2.<br>3.<br>4. | | | | |
| Excerpts | 1.<br>2.<br>3.<br>4. | | | | |
| Totals | | | | | |

| September 20, 2019 | Friday | Saturday | Sunday | Totals | Questions |
|---|---|---|---|---|---|
| Long Tones/ Scale Studies | | | | | |
| Technical Studies | | | | | |
| Etudes | | | | | |
| Repertoire | | | | | |
| Excerpts | | | | | |
| | | | | | |

| September 23, 2019 | Assignments for this week | Monday | Tuesday | Wednesday | Thursday |
|---|---|---|---|---|---|
| Long Tones/ Scale Studies | 1.<br>2.<br>3.<br>4. | | | | |
| Technical Studies | 1.<br>2.<br>3.<br>4. | | | | |
| Etudes | 1.<br>2.<br>3.<br>4. | | | | |
| Repertoire | 1.<br>2.<br>3.<br>4. | | | | |
| Excerpts | 1.<br>2.<br>3.<br>4. | | | | |
| Totals | | | | | |

| September 27, 2019 | Friday | Saturday | Sunday | Totals | Questions |
|---|---|---|---|---|---|
| Long Tones/ Scale Studies | | | | | |
| Technical Studies | | | | | |
| Etudes | | | | | |
| Repertoire | | | | | |
| Excerpts | | | | | |
| | | | | | |

| September 30, 2019 | Assignments for this week | Monday | Tuesday | Wednesday | Thursday |
|---|---|---|---|---|---|
| Long Tones/ Scale Studies | 1.<br>2.<br>3.<br>4. | | | | |
| Technical Studies | 1.<br>2.<br>3.<br>4. | | | | |
| Etudes | 1.<br>2.<br>3.<br>4. | | | | |
| Repertoire | 1.<br>2.<br>3.<br>4. | | | | |
| Excerpts | 1.<br>2.<br>3.<br>4. | | | | |
| Totals | | | | | |

| October 4, 2019 | Friday | Saturday | Sunday | Totals | Questions |
|---|---|---|---|---|---|
| Long Tones/ Scale Studies | | | | | |
| Technical Studies | | | | | |
| Etudes | | | | | |
| Repertoire | | | | | |
| Excerpts | | | | | |
| | | | | | |

| October 7, 2019 | Assignments for this week | Monday | Tuesday | Wednesday | Thursday |
|---|---|---|---|---|---|
| Long Tones/ Scale Studies | 1.<br>2.<br>3.<br>4. | | | | |
| Technical Studies | 1.<br>2.<br>3.<br>4. | | | | |
| Etudes | 1.<br>2.<br>3.<br>4. | | | | |
| Repertoire | 1.<br>2.<br>3.<br>4. | | | | |
| Excerpts | 1.<br>2.<br>3.<br>4. | | | | |
| Totals | | | | | |

| October 11, 2019 | Friday | Saturday | Sunday | Totals | Questions |
|---|---|---|---|---|---|
| Long Tones/ Scale Studies | | | | | |
| Technical Studies | | | | | |
| Etudes | | | | | |
| Repertoire | | | | | |
| Excerpts | | | | | |
| | | | | | |

| October 14, 2019 | Assignments for this week | Monday | Tuesday | Wednesday | Thursday |
|---|---|---|---|---|---|
| Long Tones/ Scale Studies | 1.<br>2.<br>3.<br>4. | | | | |
| Technical Studies | 1.<br>2.<br>3.<br>4. | | | | |
| Etudes | 1.<br>2.<br>3.<br>4. | | | | |
| Repertoire | 1.<br>2.<br>3.<br>4. | | | | |
| Excerpts | 1.<br>2.<br>3.<br>4. | | | | |
| Totals | | | | | |

| October 18, 2019 | Friday | Saturday | Sunday | Totals | Questions |
|---|---|---|---|---|---|
| Long Tones/ Scale Studies | | | | | |
| Technical Studies | | | | | |
| Etudes | | | | | |
| Repertoire | | | | | |
| Excerpts | | | | | |
| | | | | | |

| October 21, 2019 | Assignments for this week | Monday | Tuesday | Wednesday | Thursday |
|---|---|---|---|---|---|
| Long Tones/ Scale Studies | 1.<br>2.<br>3.<br>4. | | | | |
| Technical Studies | 1.<br>2.<br>3.<br>4. | | | | |
| Etudes | 1.<br>2.<br>3.<br>4. | | | | |
| Repertoire | 1.<br>2.<br>3.<br>4. | | | | |
| Excerpts | 1.<br>2.<br>3.<br>4. | | | | |
| Totals | | | | | |

| October 25, 2019 | Friday | Saturday | Sunday | Totals | Questions |
|---|---|---|---|---|---|
| Long Tones/ Scale Studies | | | | | |
| Technical Studies | | | | | |
| Etudes | | | | | |
| Repertoire | | | | | |
| Excerpts | | | | | |
| | | | | | |

| October 28, 2019 | Assignments for this week | Monday | Tuesday | Wednesday | Thursday |
|---|---|---|---|---|---|
| Long Tones/ Scale Studies | 1.<br>2.<br>3.<br>4. | | | | |
| Technical Studies | 1.<br>2.<br>3.<br>4. | | | | |
| Etudes | 1.<br>2.<br>3.<br>4. | | | | |
| Repertoire | 1.<br>2.<br>3.<br>4. | | | | |
| Excerpts | 1.<br>2.<br>3.<br>4. | | | | |
| Totals | | | | | |

| November 1, 2019 | Friday | Saturday | Sunday | Totals | Questions |
|---|---|---|---|---|---|
| Long Tones/ Scale Studies | | | | | |
| Technical Studies | | | | | |
| Etudes | | | | | |
| Repertoire | | | | | |
| Excerpts | | | | | |
| | | | | | |

| November 4, 2019 | Assignments for this week | Monday | Tuesday | Wednesday | Thursday |
|---|---|---|---|---|---|
| Long Tones/ Scale Studies | 1.<br>2.<br>3.<br>4. | | | | |
| Technical Studies | 1.<br>2.<br>3.<br>4. | | | | |
| Etudes | 1.<br>2.<br>3.<br>4. | | | | |
| Repertoire | 1.<br>2.<br>3.<br>4. | | | | |
| Excerpts | 1.<br>2.<br>3.<br>4. | | | | |
| Totals | | | | | |

| November 8, 2019 | Friday | Saturday | Sunday | Totals | Questions |
|---|---|---|---|---|---|
| Long Tones/ Scale Studies | | | | | |
| Technical Studies | | | | | |
| Etudes | | | | | |
| Repertoire | | | | | |
| Excerpts | | | | | |
| | | | | | |

| November 11, 2019 | Assignments for this week | Monday | Tuesday | Wednesday | Thursday |
|---|---|---|---|---|---|
| Long Tones/ Scale Studies | 1.<br>2.<br>3.<br>4. | | | | |
| Technical Studies | 1.<br>2.<br>3.<br>4. | | | | |
| Etudes | 1.<br>2.<br>3.<br>4. | | | | |
| Repertoire | 1.<br>2.<br>3.<br>4. | | | | |
| Excerpts | 1.<br>2.<br>3.<br>4. | | | | |
| Totals | | | | | |

| November 15, 2019 | Friday | Saturday | Sunday | Totals | Questions |
|---|---|---|---|---|---|
| Long Tones/ Scale Studies | | | | | |
| Technical Studies | | | | | |
| Etudes | | | | | |
| Repertoire | | | | | |
| Excerpts | | | | | |
| | | | | | |

| November 18, 2019 | Assignments for this week | Monday | Tuesday | Wednesday | Thursday |
|---|---|---|---|---|---|
| Long Tones/ Scale Studies | 1.<br>2.<br>3.<br>4. | | | | |
| Technical Studies | 1.<br>2.<br>3.<br>4. | | | | |
| Etudes | 1.<br>2.<br>3.<br>4. | | | | |
| Repertoire | 1.<br>2.<br>3.<br>4. | | | | |
| Excerpts | 1.<br>2.<br>3.<br>4. | | | | |
| Totals | | | | | |

| November 22, 2019 | Friday | Saturday | Sunday | Totals | Questions |
|---|---|---|---|---|---|
| Long Tones/ Scale Studies | | | | | |
| Technical Studies | | | | | |
| Etudes | | | | | |
| Repertoire | | | | | |
| Excerpts | | | | | |
| | | | | | |

| November 25, 2019 | Assignments for this week | Monday | Tuesday | Wednesday | Thursday |
|---|---|---|---|---|---|
| Long Tones/ Scale Studies | 1.<br>2.<br>3.<br>4. | | | | |
| Technical Studies | 1.<br>2.<br>3.<br>4. | | | | |
| Etudes | 1.<br>2.<br>3.<br>4. | | | | |
| Repertoire | 1.<br>2.<br>3.<br>4. | | | | |
| Excerpts | 1.<br>2.<br>3.<br>4. | | | | |
| Totals | | | | | |

| November 29, 2019 | Friday | Saturday | Sunday | Totals | Questions |
|---|---|---|---|---|---|
| Long Tones/ Scale Studies | | | | | |
| Technical Studies | | | | | |
| Etudes | | | | | |
| Repertoire | | | | | |
| Excerpts | | | | | |
| | | | | | |

| December 2, 2019 | Assignments for this week | Monday | Tuesday | Wednesday | Thursday |
|---|---|---|---|---|---|
| Long Tones/ Scale Studies | 1.<br>2.<br>3.<br>4. | | | | |
| Technical Studies | 1.<br>2.<br>3.<br>4. | | | | |
| Etudes | 1.<br>2.<br>3.<br>4. | | | | |
| Repertoire | 1.<br>2.<br>3.<br>4. | | | | |
| Excerpts | 1.<br>2.<br>3.<br>4. | | | | |
| Totals | | | | | |

Month to date total:_____

Year to date total_____

| December 6, 2019 | Friday | Saturday | Sunday | Totals | Questions |
|---|---|---|---|---|---|
| Long Tones/ Scale Studies | | | | | |
| Technical Studies | | | | | |
| Etudes | | | | | |
| Repertoire | | | | | |
| Excerpts | | | | | |
| | | | | | |

| December 9, 2019 | Assignments for this week | Monday | Tuesday | Wednesday | Thursday |
|---|---|---|---|---|---|
| Long Tones/ Scale Studies | 1.<br>2.<br>3.<br>4. | | | | |
| Technical Studies | 1.<br>2.<br>3.<br>4. | | | | |
| Etudes | 1.<br>2.<br>3.<br>4. | | | | |
| Repertoire | 1.<br>2.<br>3.<br>4. | | | | |
| Excerpts | 1.<br>2.<br>3.<br>4. | | | | |
| Totals | | | | | |

| December 13, 2019 | Friday | Saturday | Sunday | Totals | Questions |
|---|---|---|---|---|---|
| Long Tones/ Scale Studies | | | | | |
| Technical Studies | | | | | |
| Etudes | | | | | |
| Repertoire | | | | | |
| Excerpts | | | | | |
| | | | | | |

| December 16, 2019 | Assignments for this week | Monday | Tuesday | Wednesday | Thursday |
|---|---|---|---|---|---|
| Long Tones/ Scale Studies | 1.<br>2.<br>3.<br>4. | | | | |
| Technical Studies | 1.<br>2.<br>3.<br>4. | | | | |
| Etudes | 1.<br>2.<br>3.<br>4. | | | | |
| Repertoire | 1.<br>2.<br>3.<br>4. | | | | |
| Excerpts | 1.<br>2.<br>3.<br>4. | | | | |
| Totals | | | | | |

| December 20, 2019 | Friday | Saturday | Sunday | Totals | Questions |
|---|---|---|---|---|---|
| Long Tones/ Scale Studies | | | | | |
| Technical Studies | | | | | |
| Etudes | | | | | |
| Repertoire | | | | | |
| Excerpts | | | | | |
| | | | | | |

| December 23, 2019 | Assignments for this week | Monday | Tuesday | Wednesday | Thursday |
|---|---|---|---|---|---|
| Long Tones/ Scale Studies | 1.<br>2.<br>3.<br>4. | | | | |
| Technical Studies | 1.<br>2.<br>3.<br>4. | | | | |
| Etudes | 1.<br>2.<br>3.<br>4. | | | | |
| Repertoire | 1.<br>2.<br>3.<br>4. | | | | |
| Excerpts | 1.<br>2.<br>3.<br>4. | | | | |
| Totals | | | | | |

Month to date total:_____

Year to date total_____

| December 27, 2019 | Friday | Saturday | Sunday | Totals | Questions |
|---|---|---|---|---|---|
| Long Tones/ Scale Studies | | | | | |
| Technical Studies | | | | | |
| Etudes | | | | | |
| Repertoire | | | | | |
| Excerpts | | | | | |
| | | | | | |

| December 30, 2019 | Assignments for this week | Monday | Tuesday | Wednesday | Thursday |
|---|---|---|---|---|---|
| Long Tones/ Scale Studies | 1.<br>2.<br>3.<br>4. | | | | |
| Technical Studies | 1.<br>2.<br>3.<br>4. | | | | |
| Etudes | 1.<br>2.<br>3.<br>4. | | | | |
| Repertoire | 1.<br>2.<br>3.<br>4. | | | | |
| Excerpts | 1.<br>2.<br>3.<br>4. | | | | |
| Totals | | | | | |

Month to date total:_____

Year to date total_____

| January 3, 2020 | Friday | Saturday | Sunday | Totals | Questions |
|---|---|---|---|---|---|
| Long Tones/ Scale Studies | | | | | |
| Technical Studies | | | | | |
| Etudes | | | | | |
| Repertoire | | | | | |
| Excerpts | | | | | |
| | | | | | |

www.ingramcontent.com/pod-product-compliance
Lightning Source LLC
Chambersburg PA
CBHW081154180526
45170CB00006B/2084